HOW TO
STORY
GOOD NEWS

*In Worship
and Preaching*

Daniel V. Runyon

How to Story *Good News in Worship and Preaching*
By Daniel V. Runyon

Copyright 2022 by Daniel V. Runyon

ISBN: 9798402246867

Independently published by
Daniel V. Runyon
167 Burr Oak Drive
Spring Arbor, MI 49283
Contact the publisher at dvrunyon@gmail.com

Available on Amazon: $6.95

Contents

Introduction

Storying in Worship

This volume models seven dialogical worship services between God and those who long to worship him:

➤ God speaks through a call to worship; we respond with a collective prayer.

➤ God speaks through a reading from the Old Testament; we respond with a Psalm.

➤ God speaks through a New Testament letter and a gospel reading; we respond in prayer.

➤ God speaks through his Spirit; we respond with singing.

➤ God speaks into our hearts; we respond with reverence, and with tithes and offerings.

➤ God speaks through his preaching servant; we respond in obedience and—as often as we do it—by partaking of the body and blood of Christ in remembrance of him.

This ancient form of call and response dialogue with God is captured here by a series of worship services following the liturgical calendar designed to story the Good News over one calendar year.

The Advent season leads up to Christmas and is followed by Epiphany, Lent, Easter, and the Ascension, which takes up half of the year as we rehearse the story of God's sojourn on earth through the person of Jesus. Pentecost takes up the remainder of the year as we rehearse the story of God's sojourn on earth through Spirit-filled people who are the Body of Christ—the Church.

One service is provided for each of the seven major components of the year including a collective prayer and Bible texts from the Revised Common Lectionary: https://www.lectionarypage.net/. Read all scriptures aloud and note that most passages from the prophets and gospels are stories.

Sing all the verses of the suggested hymns, since to leave out a verse is like leaving out a chapter from a novel—most hymns have a plot, and those selected reinforce the theme of the service. Music for most of the hymns are available at https://hymnary.org/ or can be heard on You Tube.

The homilies are brief and meant to be read aloud as they tell a story focused on New Testament truth with Old Testament grounding.

Storying in Preaching

This pamphlet is grounded in the conviction that rehearsing the story of God is the purpose of worship. From Genesis to Revelation, the Bible tells that story.

Unlike the religious texts of most religions, full as they are of rules and maxims and dictates, the Bible is a story. Categorize all the words in the Bible and you will see the book is at least 40% narrative; some scholars say as much as 80%.

For those who say they prefer an exegetical sermon to mere storytelling, note that a story properly crafted might offer a more thorough exegesis of a passage than any didactic lecture. See for example Chapter 5 where Jesus, in dialogue with disciples on the Emmaus Road, brings alive a thrilling experiential encounter with an otherwise boring list of proof texts authenticating his identity.

So let us experiment with spending between 40% and 80% of our time in worship enjoying the story of God. Homilies can use the same techniques of the Bible—and of fiction writers. Here are some common elements of literature that make for great storying-the-Good-News preaching:

Plot: The Bible is a story with a plot—a series of events that moves the narrative along. The stage is set, characters are introduced, and conflicts develop. Action gradually builds to a climax where events take a decisive turn and conflict is resolved.

To organize plots, writers use several techniques. In *foreshadowing*, for example, the writer hints at later developments (prophesy in the Bible), thus creating interest and building suspense.

Using *flashback*, the writer interrupts the flow of events to relate happenings that occurred earlier, then resumes the narrative at or near the point of interruption. Develop the plot of your homily by answering these questions:

1. What are the key events of the Bible story you wish to elaborate? Do they unfold in a conventional way or deviate in some way?
2. Does the writer use foreshadowing or flashback? If so, for what purpose?
3. What are unique features of the plot?

4. Is this plot similar to another story with which you are familiar?
5. Select plot features to include in your interpretive version of the story.

Point of View: The Bible presents the human condition from God's point of view. Learn his point of view and you will know him. Think about the point of view of every Bible story you present:

In *first-person* narration, God himself speaks.

A *third-person* narrator stays out of the story by talking about God, not about himself. Most third-person narrators reveal the thoughts of just one character. Others, with *limited omniscience* (Job and his "comforters," for example, who wonder about things they do not understand), can explore the heads of other characters.

Many biblical writers display *full omniscience* and know everything—God has told them exactly what to say. For example, Moses writes exactly what God dictates.

In your own homilies, you might also experiment with another type of third-person narration—*dramatic*—in which your point of view moves about like a movie camera recording the actions and words of characters without revealing thoughts. Stories with surprise endings often use this technique.

Setting: Setting locates characters in time, place, and culture so they can think, feel, and act within this background. Whenever you tell a Bible story, be sure to locate details of the story in historical perspective as is done in Chapter 3, "The Leading of a Star."

Credibility is gained when hearers realize the Magi could have traveled the Silk Road from China to Babylon, a well-established route 200 years before the birth of Jesus.

Ask these questions about your setting:

1. What do you want to accomplish with the setting? You can create mood, reveal character, or use the setting in a symbolic way.
2. What research must I do to make sure the setting is realistic? Use extrabiblical historical sources to establish context and make your presentation of the truth more plausible.

Symbols: The Bible is soaked in symbolism. Every name, person, object, place, color, number, and action has significance beyond its surface meaning. Learn these symbols and point them out to your listeners so they can appreciate the profound depths of the meaning behind every word of Scripture.

Private symbols have special significance within a literary work but not outside it while *conventional* symbols are deeply rooted in culture, and almost everyone knows what they represent. Think about these questions concerning symbols:

1. What symbols are used in your source and where do they appear?
2. Are they *private* or *conventional?*
3. What do they appear to mean?
4. Do any of them undergo a change in meaning? If so, how and why?

5. Which symbol(s) could I stress in my narrative to strengthen listener comprehension of the truth being explored?

Irony: Ironic features are discrepancies between appearance and reality, expectation and outcome. Sometimes a character says one thing but means something else—possibly the exact opposite. Irony also results when one character recognizes something as important, but another character does not. If you miss the irony, you are in danger of a flawed interpretation of the intended teaching. So be sure to ask these questions regarding irony:

1. Where does irony occur?
2. What does it accomplish?
3. Why is it used?

Theme: This is the controlling idea, observation, or insight about life conditions or terms of living (such as evil, pride, love). Following the church calendar automatically provides the larger theme—the God story from Advent through Pentecost.

A more refined theme is also needed for each service, and this can often be found in the language of the Collect provided by the Lectionary (see for example https://www.lectionarypage.net/.

Many vignettes in the Bible suggest several themes—or one primary motif and additional related ones. Ask these questions:

1. What are the themes in these portions of Scripture I am studying? Are they stated or unstated? From all the possible themes you identify, select just one

to give your homily the strength to make just one firm point.
2. If stated, what elements support them?
3. If unstated, what elements create them?
4. In your introduction, point out at the outset the theme you have chosen to explore.

Characterization: Nowhere will you find more richly developed characters than in the Bible—unspeakably evil characters, gloriously righteous and noble characters, ambiguously sinister characters, major and minor characters.

Each character is developed in a way that conveys a particular message or perspective. The better you understand the characters, the more accurately you can present biblical truth. To understand characters better, ask these questions:
1. How do they behave?
2. What do they look like?
3. Where do their thoughts tend to linger?
4. What do they value in life?
5. How do they talk?
6. How do other people respond to them?
7. What are their personal habits?

From Jezebel to John the Baptist, bring these characters alive! Go and learn more about what they eat, what they wear, where they live, why they act the way they do, and through them build a rich and unforgettable narrative unfolding the story of God.

The Author

Dan Runyon grew up as a preacher's kid in four different Protestant evangelical congregations, earned a college degree in Philosophy and Religion, an MA in journalism, and a PhD in Early Modern English Literature (He is an authority on the writings of John Bunyan). He wrote professionally for 22 years, then taught writing for 20 years in a university, and now is retired yet preaches weekly in a non-denominational service for an elderly congregation.

Runyon encourages his readers to tell stories from the pulpit because it's how God tells his own story. Genesis and Exodus are one long story told by Moses. Joshua and Judges are loaded with amazing short stories, Ruth is one awesome romance, and Esther is a suspenseful nail bitter.

Samuel, Kings, Chronicles—all full of stories. Ezekiel adds allegory, animation, and pictograms, and along with Hosea and Jeremiah acts out symbolic events to help people see themselves as God sees them. And don't forget the astonishing adventure of the prophet Jonah.

Not only is Acts a story, but all the sermons within it are stories. Best of all are the parables of Jesus considered the greatest short fiction ever written—profound and concise and fascinating.

What about the three-point sermon? Runyon says, "It is useful but often boring, and with a bit of creative effort, those same points can be integrated into a narrative style that achieves greater impact."

Runyon experiments with preaching homilies with a plot for his nondenominational congregation that averages age 90. They already know about God, and about sin and salvation and sanctification. What they need now is to see more deeply into what they already know by *experiencing* and reimagining their spiritual journey and bolstering their faith to finish well. This we do each Sunday by rehearsing the Story of God together.

Acknowledgements

Scripture selections and Collects are from the Revised Common Lectionary. The calls to worship and music selections are written or chosen by worship designer M. Renée Runyon, DWS.

The seven homilies are selections from 160 services in a four-volume unpublished collection by Dan and Renée Runyon used in worship from 2019-2022: *40 Days of Worship: Rehearsing the Story of God* (Vol. 1), *Remembering the Story of God* (Vol. 2), *Receiving the Story of God* (Vol. 3), and *Considering the Story of God* (Vol. 4).

Special thanks to our gracious congregation at Vista Grande Villa in Jackson, Michigan.

Chapter 1: Advent

The Man Born to Be King III: The Tempest
(From Vol. 3: *Receiving the Story of God*)

CALL TO WORSHIP: Psalm 126

ADVENT CANDLE: Luke 2:10, 17-18; 1 Thess. 1:6; 1 Peter 1:8

COLLECT: Purify our conscience, Almighty God, by your daily visitation, that your Son Jesus Christ, at his coming, may find in us a mansion prepared for himself; who lives and reigns with you, in the unity of the Holy Spirit, one God, now and for ever. Amen.

HYMN: "How Great Our Joy!"

OLD TESTAMENT: Receive this teaching from the prophet Nathan in a portion of the Story of God recorded in 2 Samuel 7:1-11, 16.

RESPONSE: Psalm 89:1-4, 19-26

HYMN: "Angels, from the Realms of Glory"

PRAYER HYMN: "Lord, You Were Rich Beyond All Splendor"

PASTORAL PRAYER

THE LORD'S PRAYER

EPISTLE: Receive this teaching from the Book of God as is written in Romans 16:25-27.

THE GOSPEL: Receive this portion of the Story of God as recorded in Luke 1:26-38.

Homily: The Tempest

For Advent this year we have been relying heavily on the gospel of Mark, which doesn't even begin with the birth of Jesus but with the Man who was born to be King showing up at one of John's baptismal services in the Jordan River.

The commentators generally agree that the man who wrote the gospel of Mark was a close associate of the apostle Peter, and he accurately preserved the preaching of Peter in this brief and blustery gospel. So—like Peter—we plunged straight through the whole book of Mark to see how real and present the teacher, Jesus, was to Peter, how real and present the Holy Spirit he sent is to us, and how urgent it is that we receive the Man born to be King of the universe as also King of our lives.

This brings us to that very interesting phrase in our prayer for today—the collect where we asked God to purify our conscience such that the Man born to be King, "at his coming, may find *in us* a mansion prepared for *himself.*"

This prayer turns inside out the sentiments of that old song, "I've Got a Mansion Just over the Hilltop." Instead of being satisfied with just a cottage below and a little pile of silver and gold, we—by the power of the Holy Spirit working within our souls— are to be building ourselves into a mansion fit for him to live in.

If you've ever been involved in a building project, you know exactly how demanding that can be. You need a blueprint and a site plan, you need zoning clearance and a building permit, you need to compact the soil and prepare the footings. It all takes intentionality, exhausting, sweat-producing effort, and lots of time—it takes 28 days just for freshly poured concrete to cure thoroughly.

And then there's the framing—don't forget to use hurricane clips on the rafters—that's a very big deal to building inspectors these days. And you've got to do the siding, the roofing, the doors and windows, the electrical wiring, the insulating, plastering, painting, flooring—it's a huge undertaking. But even all that can usually be accomplished in a year or so.

But for him to find in us a mansion prepared for himself—that will take us a whole lifetime. The fact that we're still alive means we're not finished yet!

But we are fortunate, for the Man born to be King is a carpenter! He wants to come along beside you and guide every inch of the process. And he'll not just open your eyes to see things correctly. He'll not just open your mind to comprehend how everything fits together. He'll not just inspire you to do your best work—he'll remind you that you are building this for him! So in all your building, you don't want what you want. You want what he wants.

No wonder the gospel of Mark is such a tempestuous book. The Man born to be King arrives on the scene and finds that the *temple* the Pharisees and Sadducees and priests and other religious officials are building is a mess! They've got it all wrong! They seem to have lost track of the blueprint!

They're spending the budget on all the wrong stuff! The thing they have built is not fit for a fisherman's fish *tank*, let alone for someone of the King of Kings' *rank*!

So this tempestuous fisherman Peter narrates through Luke the story of how Jesus set the temple back on its firm foundation. That foundation is clearly indicated in our Old Testament reading. David has in mind to carry out an elaborate construction project, imaging that his rocks are good enough to accommodate God. The cedars he can import from Lebanon will smell good enough to please celestial nostrils. Maybe if he had come up with the idea of stained-glass windows—maybe then the Lord would be pleased....

How providential that the Lord came to Nathan the prophet and advised him to remind David that he was transformed from a shepherd boy to prince over Israel, and that the habitation he wants is *in the hearts* of all the people of the nation. He says, "I the Lord will make *you* a house. Your house and your kingdom shall be made sure forever before me; your throne shall be established forever."

The English is slippery here. God didn't say, "I will make *for* you a house," which suggests that David's got a mansion just over the hilltop. No, David already has a mansion right here on the hilltop in Jerusalem, the most important hilltop on our planet.

God said, "I will make *you* a house," which suggests that David and all his descendants *are* that house.

And it's not just a house to be dug up three thousand years later as an interesting archaeological dig. It's better than that. Much better. It's a house that "shall be established forever." It is the habitation Peter shows Jesus building in the gospel of Mark, crafted endlessly into perfection and ready for habitation by someone of the rank of the Man born to be King.

This truth Mark has preserved for us is rooted way back in the 2 Samuel story of Nathan's prophecy to the house of David.

No surprise then, that it's a girl from the house of David to whom the angel Gabriel was sent as we were told in Luke chapter 1. We learn that Gabriel was sent by God to a town in Galilee called Nazareth, to a virgin engaged to a man whose name was Joseph, *of the house of David.* The virgin's name was Mary, and the message clearly advances God's house-building plans.

The familiar part is that Mary has found favor with God, will conceive in her womb and bear a son, and will name him Jesus. The truly earth-shaking part is that he will be called the Son of the Most High, and the Lord God will give to him David's throne, and he will reign over the house of Jacob forever.

Let's see, Jacob is a deep ancestor of David and the grandson of Abraham who was called by God and promised that out of him would come a kingdom that would never end. Clearly, Gabriel is working from the original blueprint—this scheme is based on the true schematic, and so he delivers the somewhat redundant but profoundly significant conclusion, that the Lord God will give to him *David's* throne, and he will reign over the house of *Jacob* forever. And of his kingdom there will be no end.

Mary is from a household devoted to building into themselves a dwelling place for the Man born to be King. Amazing!—in her own womb is the first literal dwelling place fit for the baby whom she will nurture into the Man born to be King.

God surely delegates to us humans a lot of responsibility. What a spectacular house God is building—in us—as long as our response is the same as Mary's: "Here am I, the servant of the Lord; let it be with me according to your word."

Now, this job of becoming such people, that when he returns the King will find *in us* a mansion prepared for himself, is no easy task. Nobody presumes it will be easy—especially not the guys who reported this story to us. I need say nothing about Peter the tempestuous fisherman yanked from his boat to become the tempestuous disciple until the Holy Spirit at Pentecost turns him into the tempestuous preacher!

And look at this guy who has become his sidekick—John Mark. We think this is the same fellow the apostle Paul and his mentor Barnabas took with them on early missionary efforts, and when it's time to set out on another trip, Barnabas wants to bring John Mark along again. But Acts 15:38-40 says, "Paul did not think it wise to take him, because he had deserted them in Pamphylia. They had such a sharp disagreement that they parted company. Barnabas took Mark and sailed for Cyprus, but Paul chose Silas."

You should have been there! Imagine the look on Mark's face. It's like watching your parents get a divorce. Mark has known his share of conflict and tempest and failure, but he is in good hands because he has Barnabas for a mentor. And before that, he had a mom—another one of those godly women in the Bible called Mary. We know this because of the story in Acts 12: Herod has already murdered James, the brother of John, which made the Jews so happy he also tossed Peter into prison to save for execution after Passover.

An angel springs Peter from prison, escorts him out into the street and disappears. When it dawned on Peter what had just happened, it says in Acts 12, "he went to the house of Mary the mother of John, also called Mark, where many people had gathered and were praying."

This gives us insight into the long-established and respectful relationship between Peter and John Mark. In one of the greatest crises of his life, Peter entrusts his very life into the hands of the family of John Mark. John Mark is from a household that has obviously weathered a lot of tempests but is yet devoted to building into themselves a dwelling place for the Man born to be King.

Think of yourself as one of those Cape Cod houses built on the Maine coast rocks where hurricane-driven wind and crashing waves and sleet and hail hammer you. You are mighty glad to have been fashioned out of stuff built for eternity in order to become part of the great mystery of the ages—the dwelling place of God.

Paul talks about this mystery in Romans 16:25-27: That it is God who is able to strengthen you in the proclamation of Jesus Christ according to the revelation of the mystery now disclosed, and through the prophetic writings now made known even to Gentiles, to bring about the obedience of faith that can build us into a house worthy of the Man born to be King.

It's time to bring this tempestuous message to its tempestuous conclusion with a song you have probably never before sung during Advent. But listen carefully to the words and you'll see it fits perfectly. It sounds like it could have been written by Peter, or Mark, or Mary, or Paul—but this version is by Mary Ann Baker, a Baptist lady in Chicago, in 1874.

MUSICAL MEDITATION: "Master, the Tempest Is Raging"

Stylistic Observations

The Man Born to be King *radio drama by Dorothy Sayers provides the imaginative springboard and integrating theme for this homily, the third in a four-part Advent series. Titled "The Tempest" to capture the personality of Peter, it uses the building metaphor to illustrate the work of God in building his individual followers into the Body of Christ.*

Note how concise transitions weave various texts together, as in "This truth Mark has preserved for us is rooted way back in the 2 Samuel story of Nathan's prophecy to the house of David. No surprise then, that it's a girl from the house of David...."

The breezy style provides interest and aggressive pacing to get a lot said in 15 minutes, as in "Herod has already murdered James, the brother of John, which made the Jews so happy he also tossed Peter into prison to save for execution after Passover. An angel springs Peter from prison, escorts him out into the street and disappears...." Such paraphrasing and summary of the text helps the audience remember what they've heard before without bogging down the narrative.

Note also that the speaker strives to never use first person pronouns as in "I think, I believe, I know, my opinion is...." The speaker knows his own opinion is irrelevant. It is God's perspective we always seek to discover when rehearsing the story of God.

Your Notes:

_____

_____

_____

_____

_____

_____

Chapter 2: Christmas

Exile and Return
(From Vol. 2: *Remembering the Story of God*)

CALL TO WORSHIP: Psalm 145:10, 21

COLLECT: O God, who wonderfully created, and yet more wonderfully restored, the dignity of human nature: Grant that we may share the divine life of him who humbled himself to share our humanity, your Son Jesus Christ; who lives and reigns with you, in the unity of the Holy Spirit, one God, for ever and ever. Amen.

HYMN: "The Birthday of a King"

OLD TESTAMENT: Remember this prophesy from the Book we love found in Jeremiah 31:7-14.

RESPONSE: Psalm 84

HYMN: "O Worship the King"

HYMN: "A Child of the King"

PASTORAL PRAYER

THE LORD'S PRAYER

EPISTLE: Remember this teaching from the Book we love found in Ephesians 1:3-6,15-19a.

THE GOSPEL: Remember this story about Jesus from the Book we love found in Matthew 2:13-15,19-23.

Homily: Exile and Return
The scriptures we read for this second Sunday after Christmas all have as their context true stories

about exile and return. The Old Testament exiles return. The baby Jesus goes into exile into Egypt only to return when the time is right. The Wise Men deliver their gifts, satisfy their curiosity, worship the King, and return home.

In Latin America, where I used to take college students during the month of January, today is known as Three Kings Day—they make a very big deal about the wise men and their expedition to see the Christ Child.

How did these men know to make this journey? A close reading of parts of the Old Testament tells the story.

Some of the wisdom these men had was delivered to them by Daniel, the Jewish exile in Babylon who became the chief of all the wise men, counsel to Babylonian kings beginning with Nebuchadnezzar, and no doubt Daniel ruled in the place of the king when that man spent seven years of insanity living as a wild beast.

Daniel got a good bit of his wisdom from reading the books of Moses who prophesied about exile and return. Also, Daniel read the writings of his contemporary, the prophet Jeremiah, who spoke both about the 70-year Babylonian exile, and about the timing of the coming of the Messiah.

Let's look at Moses first. The very first prophecy in the Bible to foretell of the return of exiles from captivity is spoken by Moses in Deuteronomy 30:1-5. It is at the end of the first exile when Israel spent 400 years in Egypt, were brought back to the land by

Moses, and in his farewell address he tells them another exile will come. They will fall away from being faithful, God will send them into exile, and then he will bring them back.

Moses says, "When everything I've described to you has happened, and you've experienced first the blessings of obedience and then the curses for disobedience, if you reflect on these blessings and curses while you're living in the nations where the Eternal your God has scattered you; and if you and your descendants return to Him completely, heart and soul, and listen to His voice, obeying everything I've commanded you this day, then He will have mercy on you and bring you back from captivity.

"He'll gather you from all the peoples you've been scattered among. Even if you've been sent to the ends of the heavens, He will gather you together and bring you back from there to the land that belonged to your ancestors, and it will be yours once again."

That's the prophesy of Moses. Now let's notice a few things from the Jeremiah 31 passage. Jeremiah says the Lord is going to gather the remnant of Israel from the land of the north. That's odd, because Babylon is to the east, and Egypt is to the south. He adds that he will gather them, not just from the north (a place called Russia today where a lot of Jews have lived in exile), but from the farthest parts of the earth.

Jeremiah says to declare it in the coastlands far away: "He who scattered Israel will gather him, and will keep him as a shepherd a flock." The Lord has ransomed Jacob and has redeemed him from hands too strong for him. So, different parts of Jeremiah are about two different exiles—the immediate one to Babylon, plus a few who go to Egypt, and a far distant future exile that we know about since we live in that far distant future.

Daniel knew these prophesies and understood them as far as they related to the Babylonian captivity. He also had the ability to interpret dreams, a gift given directly to him from God himself. As for his own prophesies, those came to him from the angelic representatives of God who met with him in person. From these encounters, Daniel knew exactly when to expect the exiles to return from Babylon back to Jerusalem.

Also based on what Daniel wrote, the Wise Men knew precisely when to look for the One born to be King of the Jews—the One they came to worship and that we celebrate this time of the year.

But some things in the prophesies Daniel didn't understand. He admits to being confused by his own revelations. He writes in Daniel 12: 8, "I heard *what he said* but could not understand *its meaning.*" That's because he was seeing, not one, but two arrivals of the King of the Jews. Not one but two exiles and returns—the immediate one that gets the people back from Babylon and Egypt to Israel, and a future one that will gather the Jews dispersed to the ends of the earth, back to their homeland.

About the end times, the man in white linen reassures Daniel, "Many will keep themselves pure and clean and refined *despite the pressures of these times,* but those who are wicked will continue their wicked ways and none of them will *ever* understand. But those who are wise will understand."

Those who are wise will understand. Could it be that **we** are in a position to be those wise people?

This understanding that Daniel sought is easier for us because we have 2,600 years of history to look at that he didn't have. Our Western civilization has paid a lot of attention to this pattern of exile and return.

This "exile and return" pattern in history is also featured in many of the biblically informed western literary masterpieces. My colleague U. Milo Kaufmann, the gifted Milton scholar who taught at the University of Illinois at Urbana, recognizes this pattern in the biblical narrative of Jacob—who leaves the Promised Land for Egypt, and the nation of Israel that descended from him returns to the same land centuries later.

The pattern turns up in Herman Melville's book *Moby Dick*, Hemingway's *Old Man and the Sea*, and in J. R. R. Tolkien's *The Hobbit,* which even carries the subtitle *There and Back Again.*

There is a qualitative difference at the new beginning. Experience results in wisdom, or contentment, or an enriched understanding of the value of a possession. The protagonist has attained new levels of moral and intellectual development. Like Job, he is *willing* to suffer.

The prophecy for Adam and his seed is that "God shall wipe away all tears from their eyes; and there shall be no more death, neither sorrow, nor crying, neither shall there be any more pain: for the former things are passed away. And he that sat upon the throne said, Behold, I make all things new" (Rev. 21:4-5a).

Adam had his beginning in Eden, and he is back again, only now he is a better man with a deeper appreciation for all he has been given, and a deep understanding of all he has experienced.

In literature, in scripture, and in the history of the world we see this theme of exile and return. The wise men saw this, and nothing mattered more than for them to go on pilgrimage, "for we have seen his star, and have come to worship."

Wise men still seek him. And if there were people today as wise as the wise men of old, they would be equally knowledgeable about coming events.

They would know about the Year of Jubilee concept taught in Leviticus 25 where Moses explains that at the end of each 50-year period, the people are supposed to be able to return to their land, all debts are to be cancelled, all slaves are to be freed—after exile there is always return.

In addition to their astronomy skills, the wise men who went on pilgrimage to see the baby Jesus were probably historians like the modern-day Rabbi Jonathan Cahn. He has noticed things in the past 2,000 years as obvious as the things the wise men knew from the 2,000 years that preceded them.

For example, Rabbi Cahn has noticed that the year was AD 67 when the Roman emperor Nero sent Vespasian to invade Israel from the north, beginning in Galilee. That is when the great, end-time exile revealed to Daniel had its beginning.

Based on the 50-year Jubilee concept, Rabbi Cahn says you can count every 50th year from then to now as a year of jubilee. If you add up 29 bunches of 50 years each, that brings you to the year 1517. That was the year when the land of Israel became part of the Ottoman Empire—it was conquered by Muslims—and that was the last land transfer before the more recent times of restoration.

Can't you just imagine those three wise men putting their headss together and saying, "Ok, now let's jump forward another 350 years, or seven sets of 50-year jubilees. Where would that put us?"

Balthazar takes out his calculator and says, "Hey! That takes us to 1867, or the 36th Jubilee." He glances at Caspar and says, "did anything important happen in 1867?"

"You betcha!" says **Caspar.** "That's when the most recent return to the land of Israel had its beginning. In 1867 a stranger named Mark Twain visited Israel while writing his book *Innocents Abroad.*"

"Interesting coincidence!" chimes in **Melchior.** "Because the prophesies in Scripture speak both about a stranger, and also about a man with a measuring line. And 1867 is also the year when the man with the measuring line came to the former country called Israel and discovered the ancient, lost city of Jerusalem." I think it's safe to say that would be Charles Warren, the British officer and member of the Royal Engineers who surveyed the whole place starting in 1867."

"Righto!" says **Caspar**. "That's a well-known historical fact—that's when the lost city of Jerusalem was rediscovered, and archaeological excavation began."

Balthazar is still staring at his calculator and now he says, "Think about this: Fifty years after 1867 brings us to 1917. By my calculations, that would be the 37th Jubilee, which just so happens to fall at the end of the First World War."

A lightbulb goes off in the brain of our English history scholar **Melchior** and he says, "Hmmm, that's when the leading world power at that time, the British under Allenby, drove out the Ottoman Empire and gave the land of Israel to the Jewish people."

Caspar says, "You're making me wonder what happens 50 years after that."

Balthazar doesn't even need his abacas to add 50 years to 1917. He just says, "Fifty years after 1917 puts us in 1967, on the 38th Jubilee...."

Melchior interrupts, almost shouting, "Shazaam! Everybody knows that's when the Jewish soldiers entered the gates of Jerusalem, and the Israeli nation was born in the Six-Day War!"

By this time Balthazar, Caspar, and Melchior are looking at each other in astonishment, because their brains are jumping forward another 50 years, and it brings them to 2017.

Fresh in their memories is the <u>fact</u> that on the 39th Jubilee from the year of the Vespasian invasion of Israel, the leader of the greatest world power at that time was an American named Donald <u>Trump</u> who recognized Jerusalem as the capital of Israel, and he made a rather unpopular political move and established the American embassy in Jerusalem.

Interestingly, these wise men have been around long enough to have learned the meaning of words— like the word "Trump," short for "trumpet," or one who spouts off loudly, like the Jewish shofar or ram's horn trumpet. And they would know that the word "Donald" means "world leader."

All you have just heard is exactly the sort of information the Three Wise Men—the three biblically informed historians, would have had access to if they had lived—like we have—in 21st century.

Being the sort of thinkers and the savvy logicians they no doubt were—I can now see them looking into our future.

Balthazar speaks for all of them when he says, "Let's see. Every 50 years something really significant seems to happen. The prophesies of Moses and Jeremiah and Daniel about exile and return have all turned out to be true. We see a pattern here. Throughout history, the people of God are driven out of the land of Israel, only to return.

"In this most recent exile after the crucifixion we see that Jesus, the King of the Jews, was the first to leave the land—he ascended into heaven. Then the Roman invasion obliterated that nation, and everybody was scattered to the ends of the earth.

"Conditions changed in 1867 and things were set in motion so the land could be given back to them. In 1917 the land actually was given back but was not fully theirs until 50 years later when, in 1967, they won the Six Day War.

"So they had their land, and they had their nation, but they did not have their capital until 2017 when the world leader of that time loudly announced that he recognized Jerusalem and restored to them their ancient City of David."

Caspar says, "What's left to return? Only one thing—the Return of the King! Must be that is scheduled for the next Jubilee—which in coming in 2067. Perhaps then is when the King of the Jews will return."

Melchior slaps his leg and says, "That'll be a Three Kings Day worth celebrating!"

"Read the prophesies again," says Balthazar. "That'll be the biggest wedding celebration ever."

Here's an interesting side note. It is said in scripture that while no man knows precisely the day or hour of the Lord's return—just that it will be the Day of Judgment—we do know that in Jewish culture, the biggest celebration of their year is known as Rosh Hashanah.

Rosh Hashanah was ordained as the Day of Judgment for all of mankind because it is believed that on this day the creation of the world was completed, and it was the Divine intention that the world be ruled by justice—by a Prince of Peace. The Day of Judgment is also the Jewish New Year festival and features the blowing of the shofar.

The next Jubilee Year will be 2067. Rosh Hashanah in that year will be Friday Sept 9 (Rosh Hashanah Eve), through Rosh Hashanah Day on Saturday, September 10 which is the Jewish Sabbath, and it will end on Rosh Hashana Day 2 on Sunday, September 11, the Christian day of worship.

The Day of the Lord's return will be the wedding day of the Lamb for all who are his. The Church, the Body of Christ, as well as all those Jews who are prophesied to be grafted back into the tree—this Church is the bride that will be united to Jesus at the marriage supper of the Lamb.

You may feel this idea is a bit far-fetched because Paul did write in 1 Thessalonians 5:2 that "the day of the Lord will come like a thief in the night." But he finishes the thought two sentences later in verses four and five where he says, "But you, brothers and sisters, are not in darkness so that this day should surprise you like a thief. You are all children of the light and children of the day."

Well anyway—regardless of when it happens, everybody is invited to the wedding feast of the marriage supper of the Lamb. You are invited. The innkeeper will be there. The shepherds will be there. The three wise guys will certainly know to be there—and they'll be bearing gifts—because they'll be looking for Jesus, who most certainly will be there.

You won't have any trouble recognizing the King on his White Horse.

Be wise: begin now to prepare yourself as a gift to offer the King of Kings on his great wedding day.

CLOSING HYMN: "Lo, He Comes with Clouds Descending"

Stylistic Observations

The first part of this homily adopts the same breezy narrative style as the previous chapter to acquaint the audience with how the various Bible texts concerning exile and return fit together. The literary influence of contemporary scholars U. Milo Kaufmann and Rabbi Jonathan Cahn are explained in journalistic style as part of the narrative.

Imagined dialogue between three wise men is intentionally riddled with humor to underscore the speculative nature of the material while triggering audience engagement as to future possibilities: "Can't you just imagine those three wise men putting their heads together and saying, 'Ok, now let's jump forward another 350 years....'"

Your Notes:

_____

_____

_____

_____

_____

_____

Chapter 3: Epiphany

The Leading of a Star
(From Vol. 4: *Considering the Story of God*)

CALL TO WORSHIP: Psalms 61, 43, 139, 143

COLLECT: O God, by the leading of a star you manifested your only Son to the peoples of the earth: Lead us, who know you now by faith, to your presence, where we may see your glory face to face; through Jesus Christ our Lord, who lives and reigns with you and the Holy Spirit, one God, now and for ever. Amen.

HYMN: "God of the Ages, Whose Almighty Hand"

OLD TESTAMENT: Consider the joyful hope for the world prophesied in Isaiah 60:1-6.

RESPONSE: Psalm 72:1-7,10-14

HYMN: "From All That Dwell Below the Skies"

PRAYER HYMN: "As with Gladness Men of Old"

PASTORAL PRAYER

THE LORD'S PRAYER

EPISTLE: Consider this good news for Gentiles as explained by Paul in Ephesians 3:1-12.

THE GOSPEL: Consider this report of some travelers who showed up in Jerusalem as reported in Matthew 2:1-12.

Homily: The Leading of a Star

When I was a college professor I either taught a fiction writing class during January or led cross cultural studies classes overseas. In some of those places, people call this Sunday "Three Kings Day," and I have experienced it celebrated in dramatic ways in South Korea, Puerto Rico, and Peru. The pageantry, the fireworks, the joyful reenactments celebrate the extravagant extent to which the Wise Men went to see the glory of God face to face.

In this homily I combine a narrative of international travel with some imaginings that fit the category of historical fiction. That is to say, the event really happened, the characters were real people, but we must use our imagination to string the events likely to have happened into a plausible narrative. In so doing, perhaps you'll experience a profound insight of your own, suitable for this first Sunday of Epiphany.

I'd first like take you to China where archives of historical literature reveal remarkable facts about the distant past—legends handed down since the dawn of time about Creation, a worldwide flood, and a family who survived by finding refuge in a large boat (Paul Hattaway, *Back to Jerusalem,* p. 1 & following).

These ancient people in regions that today we call China had a deep reverence for the Creator God who reigned supreme over the affairs of mankind, and who they refused to represent by an image or idol. As they developed their written language, they wove into many written Chinese characters biblical stories and principles.

A tradition that lasted for centuries involved the emperor offering annual sacrifices to *Shangdi*, the Heavenly Emperor. (Until recently, Protestant Christians in China used the name *Shangdi* for God.) The prayer to Shangdi recited annually by the emperor reads as follows:

> *Of old in the beginning, there was great chaos, without form and dark. The five elements (planets) had not begun to evolve, nor the sun and moon to shine. In the midst thereof there existed neither form nor sound.*
>
> *You, O Spiritual Sovereign, came forth in your presidency, and first did divide the grosser part from the purer. You made heaven; You made earth; You made man. All things with their reproducing power got their beginning.*
>
> *To thee, O mysteriously working Maker, I look up in thought.... With the great ceremonies I reverently honor Thee. Thy servant, I am but a reed or willow; my heart is but that of an ant; yet have I received Thy favoring decree, appointing me to the government of the empire.*
>
> *I deeply cherish a sense of my ignorance and blindness, and am afraid lest I prove unworthy of Thy great favors. Therefore will I observe all the rules and statutes, striving, insignificant as I am, to discharge my loyal duty. For distant here, I look up to Thy heavenly palace.*

Come in Thy precious chariot to the altar.
Thy servant, I bow my head to the earth
reverently, expecting Thine abundant grade.... O
that thou wouldest accept our offerings, and
regard us, while thus we worship Thee, whose
goodness is inexhaustible!

Of course, before offering such a prayer the emperor was carefully dressed in his gold-threaded dragon robes that were a symbol of his own supreme power—the dragon being a composite of the best parts of other animals: an eagles' claws, a lion or tiger's teeth and head, a snake's body, and wings for flying. The dragon's role is symbolic of magic, of power and supremacy, and the emperors adopted this symbolism.

The chief astrologer at court, a man named Liu Shang, would not think to wear such clothing, and anyway he vastly preferred his comfortable and versatile *Hànfú* outfit. Perfect for stargazing in the cold night, it featured a crossing collar, waistband, and a right-hand lapel. Adaptable for any weather from sweltering heat to stifling cold, it featured layers of shirts, jackets, robes, skirts, and trousers.

Liu Shang's clothing was proven gear introduced by the Han Dynasty 200 years before Christ and would be worn another 200 years after Christ. Liu Shang liked his silver adornments of blue Kingfisher feathers, blue gems, glass, and especially the jade suitable to his rank, valuing it for its hardness, and durability, and because its beauty increased with time. If need be, it could also be used as money.

Indeed, Liu Shang was rubbing a jade button between the thumb and middle finger of his right hand that crisp, bright winter night when he spotted the anomaly in the constellations that utterly astonished him. He rechecked its location numerous times, compared it with his charts, consulted with his students, and determined that knowledge of this amazing discovery should be taken to the emperor.

It was just last week that the emperor had prayed the annual prayer to Shangdi, and when he received word of a newly born emperor star, he determined to spare no expense to organize an expedition to be led by Liu Shang to learn what more he could about this anomaly in space.

"Prepare for a long journey," the emperor commanded Liu Shang. "It will take at least a year—very likely two years if my guess is correct—to reach your destination. Our next Silk Road Caravan leaves the morning after the coming New Moon. Travel with them, study this 'emperor star' every night, and follow where it leads—no matter whether it takes you to India or Arabia or the Horn of Africa. As you know, it is no difficulty for me to ensure safe travel wherever the star takes you—we have maintained these trade routes for two centuries, and under my watch it shall be strengthened all the more."

The emperor paused to study the excited face of his highly prized astronomer as if to discern his thoughts. Then he said, "Ah! And what if you should succeed? We must send gifts! Anything in our vast treasury is at your disposal. What will you require?"

"Your excellency," Liu Shang replied, "the gifts must first be worthy of Shangdi Himself should the star lead me to him. And yet they must be easily transported."

"Well spoken!" cried the emperor. "We must consult with the Chief Treasurer and take his counsel."

The Chief Treasurer had already heard rumors of the discovery of what they were calling the Emperor Star and made this suggestion: "We must certainly send a gift of gold. It is a compact store of value, far more easily transported than bulkier items. Iit is valuable, beautiful, and long-lasting—and we hope to hail an emperor representing Shangdi Himself. And if the mission fails, it is readily traded for other things we need."

"Gold it will be," said the emperor. "What else?"

"I have laid by a very valuable supply of frankincense," offered the treasurer. "It is reserved for use in our temple routines, but if you truly do encounter Shangdi, nothing would be more eloquent in recognizing his priesthood. As is well known, this fragrance also has medicinal qualities that Shangdi will surely value for both enhancing his healing powers while ensuring his own vibrant health."

"Well spoken," said the emperor, "we will offer him frankincense. And a third gift must be offered to show Shangdi our deep gratitude and respect."

Liu Shang had stood by quietly all this time, but now he made to speak, tentatively suggesting: "Your excellency, if this Emperor Star is what I think it is," he began—his voice quavering—"then you must know the meaning of the ancient prophecies. The reason we always say, 'Long live the emperor,' is because we fear the emperor will one day die. If *this* emperor is truly Shangdi, then he must die and conquer death—in order to conquer the ruler of the underworld and rule supreme as the One God of heaven."

The emperor squinted narrowly at Liu Shang while the treasurer searched his store of knowledge and said, "Well then, something not usually fitting as a gift might be appropriate for this all-knowing One. We must offer him myrrh."

"Myrrh!" barked the emperor. "You mean to make a gift of the embalming ointment reserved for *my* burial? You think Shangdi can be mummified?!"

When the emperor barks, everyone falls silent. But after a time, the astronomer lifted his head and said, "Your excellency, truly it would be a bittersweet gift. Every time he remembered the gift, he would remember his destiny. It might help him to be everlastingly loving and kind—and at the practical level, when he does die and is anointed for burial, who is to say but whether the myrrh will prove useful during his visit to the underworld."

"Enough said," replied the emperor. He studied the dragons embroidered in silk on both arms of his tunic. He understood the discrete references to the "ruler of the underworld" and soon found himself musing out loud, "If he is to conquer the dragon, then he is a greater emperor than I, and it behooves me to pray the annual prayer to Shangdi not just every year, but every day. Send along with Liu Shang enough myrrh to embalm a god-man."

So it was that Liu Shang left the magnificent capital city of Chang'an (today's Xi'an), traveling westward into Gansu Province through Lanzhou and other regions along the Hexi Corridor to the giant barrier of the Great Wall and the bright pearl on the ancient Silk Road, the city called Dunhuang.

From there the Silk Road broke into three main routes and Liu Shang had to study the heavens long and thoughtfully before making his choice. Should he take the southern route that ran west along the northern foot of the Kunlun Mountains, and over the Pamirs to India, and then if necessary to pass through Central Asia to reach the coast of the Mediterranean or Arabia?

Or should he choose the central route meandering west along the southern foot of the Tianshan Mountains, passing through Loulan, Korla, Chucha, and Aksu, then across the Pamirs into Russia?

The third option, the northern route, rambled along the northern foot of the Tianshan Mountains, starting at Hami and winding westward until it reached the Ili River Valley and then the Black Sea.

No matter what route he took, every day Liu Shang would thank his lucky stars that he wore the comfortable and versatile _Hànfú_ outfit, because all three Silk Road routes ran between mountain ranges and along edges of deserts, going through oases inhabited by ancient tribes.

Thanks to being thoroughly prepared, it truly was Emperor Star guidance and not his preference for comfort that he selected the southern route going west along the northern foot of the Kunlun Mountains, and over the Pamirs to India, and then, if necessary, to pass through Central Asia to reach the coast of the Mediterranean or Arabia.

Liu Shang was actually uncertain whether this was the right choice, but decided it was his best route because it would take him through Varanasi on the banks of the river Ganges in India, an important industrial center famous for its muslin and silk fabrics, perfumes, ivory works, and sculpture. He knew this was near where Buddha had given his first sermon 500 years ago, "The Setting in Motion of the Wheel of Dharma." And he would be there for some time due to all the bartering that would take place by others in his caravan, so he would have a few days to seek out scholars and discuss the Star.

Some months later he finally arrived, and he found the scholars—found out that although they were pleased when he pointed out to them the new star and listened politely to his interpretation of what it meant, they could add nothing to his knowledge.

But a fellow named Gaspar trailed him as he set out to return to the caravan. Sensing he was being followed, Liu Shang stopped, turned, and recognized Gaspar as the poor Indian scholar who had served as his translator.

"Yes?" He inquired. "What is it you seek?"

"I long to know more of this emperor star," Gaspar said. "I long to join you on this quest, only...."

Liu Shang smiled knowingly. He discerned the shabby nature of the scholar's attire. He sensed also a deep humility suggesting it was not wealth the man sought, but wisdom. "Only you can't afford to travel?" Liu Shang bluntly asked.

The mere posture of the student told him he had guessed correctly, and before he could reply, Liu Shang offered, "if you desire to join me in this grand quest, I desire to hire you to accompany me through these regions where I understand half of what I see and nothing of what I hear. Gather up whatever personal effects you may have, and I shall purchase anything you lack."

Half a year later, Gaspar and Liu Shang arrived in Babylon, which had stood for six centuries as the western anchor of the Silk Road and looked to be the end of this so-far-unsuccessful journey.

The caravan would be here for weeks, Gaspar understood the local dialect no better than Liu Shang, so they found in the marketplace and hired a local translator, told him of his mission, and he promptly took them to a Jewish synagogue where a scripture reading from Isaiah utterly astonished Liu Shang.

He almost fainted when he heard the final sentences of the reading: "Your heart shall thrill and rejoice, because the abundance of the sea shall be brought to you, the wealth of the nations shall come to you."

Liu Shang understood this to be a prophesy given a hundred years before Buddha preached his first sermon and some 400 years before the Silk Road—which it was clearly describing—had achieved its current tollroad-like status.

And then—later in the same prophesy—imagine his astonishment to hear the actions of he, himself personally—being described in the ancient prophesy: "A multitude of camels shall cover you…. They shall bring gold, and frankincense, and shall proclaim the praise of the Lord."

"Are you okay?" asked the translator as Liu Shang collapsed to his knees.

The old Chinaman raised his eyes to the heavens and proclaimed, "I have never been better!" Then he bowed his head to the floor and laughed and wept as he worshipped the great—the one and only Shangdi.

When he spoke next, the translator was saying, "Now they are reciting a Psalm written by their greatest king—David, who lived 1,000 years ago. They are saying, 'Give the King your justice, O God, and your righteousness to the King's Son; that he may rule your people righteously and the poor with justice…. He shall rescue the poor and crush the oppressor.

"'He shall live as long as the sun and moon endure, from one generation to another. In his time shall the righteous flourish; there shall be abundance of peace till the moon shall be no more. The kings of Tarshish and of the isles shall pay tribute, and the kings of Arabia and Saba offer gifts. All kings shall bow down before him, and all the nations do him service.'"

Liu Shang trembled to hear these words. He sat as if hypnotized through the entire time of worship and seemed in no hurry to leave at the end.

After the dismissal and as people drifted away, the Rabbi's eyes grew very large indeed when he saw the value of the offering left by the Chinese trader. He hastened to catch up with the wealthy foreigner and said, "Please, I must speak with you. I must invite you to have a meal with me."

When the translator made clear to Liu Shang what was being said, a wide smile broke out on his face, he bowed every bit as respectfully as he bowed to his emperor, and he said through tears, "And I must speak to you!"

And what a conversation they had, for the Rabbi opened to him the scriptures concerning the Messiah, the King of the Jews who he was expecting to come to earth, and the astronomer told the Rabbi about the Emperor Star and that he sensed he was nearing the end of his quest, and the Rabbi told him of the famous Persian astronomer named Melchior with whom he could possibly arrange a meeting.

Liu Shang offered to host any such meeting, and when a time was set, he rented a private room in Babylon's finest restaurant where they served a four-course meal featuring a choice of barley and leek soup or almond and flax soup, followed by a choice of barley salad, cucumber-pistachio salad, or sweet and sour salad. The entree course offered lamb, duck, or the vegan option, an ancient grain called "emmer." For the dessert course they enjoyed spiced emmer cake and "mersu," a combination of dates and nuts served three ways.

Melchior showed up at the restaurant with a visiting scholar from Arabia in tow. This fellow named Balthazar was effusive with enthusiasm about a new star he had just "discovered," and when he learned Liu Shang had been following it for a year he bowed in deep respect and proclaimed, "From you I have a great deal to learn!"

They talked for hours! You would have thought it was a college reunion of classmates from 50 years ago. How they talked! And when they had learned everything they possibly could from Liu Shang, the rabbi leaped up from the table and said with conviction, "You must go to Jerusalem! All of you! I can show you the way! I can take you to King Herod!"

And that is how it very likely happened that, "in the time of King Herod, after Jesus was born in Bethlehem of Judea, wise men from the East came to Jerusalem, asking, "Where is the child who has been born king of the Jews? For we observed his star at its rising, and have come to pay him homage."

With the knowledge gained from Herod "they set out; and there, ahead of them, went the star that they had seen at its rising, until it stopped over the place where the child was. "They were overwhelmed with joy, entered the house, saw the child with Mary his mother, and they knelt down and worshipped him. Then, opening their treasure chests, they offered him gifts of gold, frankincense, and myrrh.

CLOSING HYMN: HYMN: "We Three Kings"

Stylistic Observations

This narrative explains itself in the introduction and blends factual history with contrived dialogue to give Christian tradition regarding the origins of the wise men plausibility and a sense of urgency. Because it has already been introduced in this way, the speaker is free to make interjections such as "(today's Xi'an)," an explanation unlikely to be used in a true short story.

The pacing is at first leisurely as it creates the setting, then builds suspense by increasing the pace of travel until it accelerates into the climactic gospel text itself of their arrival in Bethlehem. This accelerated conclusion is called an "ellipsis" as was used by Joseph Conrad in Heart of Darkness *where, after a long journey, the first-person narrator becomes extremely ill, and the reader is swiftly transported back to civilization by the simple phrase, "I found myself back in the sepulchral city."*

My conclusion is first designed to give the listeners (who are sitting in church and watching the clock) a sense of relief, but far more importantly gives them their own epiphany into the courage, persistence, and faith of these first Gentile worshipers of Jesus.

Your Notes:

_____

_____

_____

_____

_____

Chapter 4: Lent

Water Cooler Religion
(From Vol. 2: *Remembering the Story of God*)

CALL TO WORSHIP: Psalm 5:7-8: I

COLLECT: O God, whose glory it is always to have mercy: Be gracious to all who have gone astray from your ways, and bring them again with penitent hearts and steadfast faith to embrace and hold fast the unchangeable truth of your Word, Jesus Christ your Son; who with you and the Holy Spirit lives and reigns, one God, for ever and ever. Amen.

HYMN: "Come, Thou Almighty King"

OLD TESTAMENT: Remember this story from the Book we love as recorded in Genesis 12:1-4.

RESPONSE: Psalm 121

HYMN: "Moment by Moment"

PASTORAL PRAYER

THE LORD'S PRAYER

EPISTLE: Remember this teaching from the Book we love written by the Apostle Paul to believers in Rome: Romans 4:1-5, 13-17.

THE GOSPEL: Remember this story of Jesus from the Book we love found in John 3:1-17.

Homily: Watercooler Religion

Nicodemus was one of the Sanhedrin, the ruling body of the Pharisees. He was frequently present around 10:00 a.m. when everybody took a 15-minute break to loiter by the water cooler and argue.

Around the time when Nicodemus decided to visit Jesus, the Pharisees at the water cooler were in hot debate as to whether Jesus was the Messiah. The general consensus was that he was not, and therefore they might need to do the responsible thing—something drastic to make sure Jesus didn't mislead too many people.

Nicodemus listened in but didn't say much—just thinking deeply about these things. His deep thoughts always involved searching the scriptures. While the other pharisees were arguing about all the out-and-out prophesies about the Messiah, he was thinking about their actual history—events from their past that might also reveal what would happen in the unfolding of the whole story of the messiah.

He may very well have been remembering the story of Joseph recorded in Genesis 37 and wondered if what happened to Joseph would also happen to Jesus. You will remember that Jacob loved Joseph more than any of his other kids, because he was the son of his old age; and he had made him a long, colorful robe that even had sleeves.

When his brothers stood around their water cooler and noticed that Joseph was their father's favorite, they muttered under their breaths about how unfair this was—and they began to realize they might need to do the responsible thing—something drastic to make sure Joseph didn't let this go to his head. The Bible reports they hated him, and could not speak peaceably to him.

Just like the Pharisee friends of Nicodemus, the brothers of Joseph were looking for a chance. That chance came when the brothers went to pasture their father's flock near Shechem. And Israel said to Joseph, "Are not your brothers pasturing the flock at Shechem? Come, I will send you to them."

Joseph answered, "Here I am—I have come to do your will."

The Father said to the beloved son, "Go now, see if it is well with your brothers and with the flock; and bring word back to me."

So Joseph went after his brothers, and found them—it was coffee break time and they were standing around the water cooler at Dothan. When they saw him from a distance, they also saw that this was the opportunity to execute their conspiracy—and they conspired to kill him.

They said to one another, "Here comes this dreamer. Come now, let us kill him." But as you know, instead they tossed him into a pit, sat around and thought it over, and later sold him as a slave to a caravan of Ishmaelite traders coming from Gilead on their way down to Egypt.

They sold him to the Ishmaelites for twenty pieces of silver. And the Ishmaelites took Joseph to Egypt. Nicodemus would have known the whole story of how the favored son later became the savior of the entire nation while graciously forgiving and loving the brothers who abused him.

Nicodemus was thinking, "Maybe Jesus is another Joseph—or maybe not. I know! I'll go ask him and find out!"

The next morning at the water cooler, Nicodemus heard more scuttlebutt about Jesus, and it troubled him because in his devotions he had been reading Jeremiah 18, and the story about the potter and the clay was fresh in his mind:

> The word that came to Jeremiah from the Lord: "Go down to the potter's house, and there I will let you hear my words." So Jeremiah went down to the potter's house and there watched as a clay vessel the potter was making was spoiled in his hand, and he reworked it into another vessel.

> Then the word of the Lord came to him: "Can I not do with you, O house of Israel, just as this potter has done? Just like the clay in the potter's hand, so are you in my hand. At one moment I may declare concerning a nation that I will pluck up and break down and destroy it, but if that nation, concerning which I have spoken, turns from its evil, I will change my mind about the disaster that I intended to bring on it.

> "And at another moment I may declare concerning a nation or a kingdom that I will build and plant it, but if it does evil in my sight, not listening to my voice, then I will change my

mind about the good that I had intended to do to it.

"Now, therefore, say to the people of Judah and the inhabitants of Jerusalem: Thus says the Lord: Look, I am a potter shaping evil against you and devising a plan against you. Turn now, all of you from your evil way, and amend your ways and your doings."

Then they said, "Come, let us make plots against Jeremiah—for instruction shall not perish from the priest, nor counsel from the wise, nor the word from the prophet. Come, let us bring charges against him, and let us not heed any of his words."

Nicodemus noticed that these next words out of the mouth of Jeremiah could well have been spoken by Joseph when he was down in his pit breathing radon gas and very chilly and fearing for his life: "Give heed to me, O Lord, and listen to what my adversaries say! Is evil a recompense for good? Yet they have dug a pit for my life. Remember how I stood before you to speak good for them, to turn away your wrath from them."

Something like alarm bells were going off in the mind of Nicodemus. "My goodness!" he thought, "We had better *not* do to Jesus what they did to Joseph! We had better *not* do to Jesus what they did to Jeremiah! If we do, we could experience the same punishments as they received: poverty and drought followed by exile—just as happened so many times in our past."

And then the words of Daniel 9 came to mind. As a teacher of the law, perhaps it was just last week when Nicodemus had been teaching his students about prayer and had quoted a portion of what Daniel said to God when he was fasting and praying and repenting:

> Righteousness is on your side, O Lord, but open shame, as at this day, falls on us, the people of Judah, the inhabitants of Jerusalem, and all Israel, those who are near and those who are far away, in all the lands to which you have driven them, because of the treachery that they have committed against you.

> Open shame, O Lord, falls on us, our kings, our officials, and our ancestors, because we have sinned against you. To the Lord our God belong mercy and forgiveness, for we have rebelled against him, and have not obeyed the voice of the Lord our God by following his laws, which he set before us by his servants the prophets.

So Nicodemus did go talk to Jesus, and Jesus said things too tough for even a scholar like Nicodemus to understand: Jesus told him he had to be born again! Back then, those words were not a cliché that got kicked around at 10:00 a.m. at the water cooler. As far as we know, nobody before had ever said these words: "You must be born again." Preposterous!

But there was instant interest! When will there be an IPO? Can I buy into "Born Again" stock on the ground floor? What kind of dividends will it pay?!

After startling Nicodemus with the new idea of being born both of flesh and of the spirit, Jesus took him to the next level and said something Nicodemus already understood: "As Moses lifted up the serpent in the wilderness, so must the Son of Man be lifted up, that whoever believes in him may have eternal life."

If you thought alarm bells were going off in the head of Nicodemus before, you should have heard them now! Jesus *told* this Pharisee He himself would die for the sins of the world—just as those who looked at the serpent Moses lifted up were saved from death by snake bite. Only now we're talking about Death by the Big Serpent—the one who deceived Eve and Adam in the garden.

Nicodemus realized it was his friends at the water cooler who would lift Jesus up on that cross of crucifixion—acting exactly like the older brothers of Joseph who thought they were sending their brother to certain death.

Nicodemus was already sort of expecting the Pharisees would do this, he just didn't know Jesus already knew. But then Jesus said another thing Nicodemus didn't expect—that Jesus planned to provide himself as a *voluntary* sacrifice:

"For God so loved the world that he gave his only Son, so that everyone who believes in him may not perish but may have eternal life. Indeed, God did not send the Son into the world to condemn the world, but in order that the world might be saved through him."

Wow! What secrets were stored up that day in the vast mind of Nicodemus! Everything foreshadowed in all those Hebrew scriptures that cluttered his cerebellum were going to be fulfilled in his front yard and in his lifetime!

Walking home from that private interview with Jesus, Nicodemus exclaimed, "Father Abraham! What am I going to do with what I know? What am I going to say about Jesus to the boys at the water cooler?"

Not surprisingly, Father Abraham answered using words already in the brain of Nicodemus from Genesis 12. The same thing that was true of Abraham is also true of Jesus: "I will bless those who bless you, and the one who curses you I will curse; and in you all the families of the earth shall be blessed."

Nicodemus went home and found his wife in the kitchen stirring stew. He joined her and stewed about everything he had been thinking. She listened, and listened, and listened, until both *stewings* were done.

Then she raised her wooden spoon into the air like the prophet she was and proclaimed, "It has ever been so! Some of the children of Abraham are of the synagogue of Satan; others of us are of the synagogue of the true God and the Messiah he will send."

Nicodemus was familiar with these fits of hers. He stepped back, folded his hands in that usual way of his, and said, "What else are you seeing?"

A glassy gleam came into her eye and she sayid, "It has ever been so—and it shall always be so! I see a year called Two Thousand and Eighteen when someone called a Presbyterian Minister's Wife named

Rosaria Butterfield will write a book about hospitality called *The Gospel Comes with a House Key* published by a printer called 'Crossway Books'"—

Nicodemus interrupted: "What an odd name! Books about the Way of the Cross! Are you saying this persecution of the type carried out by Romans finds its way into the future?"

"Yes!" said Golda. "And the Presbyterian lady writes on page 140, 'Many churches have cultivated the making of a Judas. They have lost their way. They think themselves more merciful than God. They think the Bible is too severe, asks too much of people. They produce Judases in their seminaries, they place them in their pulpits, and they replicate them in their pews....'"

Nicodemus sucked in his breath and said, "I know a Judas! He swings the coin bag at his side in the company of Jesus...."

Golda seemed not to hear him and just keep on quoting Butterfield who wrote, "The lesson is this: 'Neutrality is a forlorn position. He that enters but half-way into the prevailing tendency of the present day, finishes his course before he is aware that he is in the snare of the devil'" (quoting Krummacher, *Suffering Saviour*, 68-69).

Then she let go of her wooden spoon and took his face in her hands.

"Poor Nicky," she whispered. "You are just going to have to make a decision, aren't you? You are going to have to take a leap of faith like Father Abraham and bless the suffering servant who is blessed by God, or you can become complicit with the water cooler club and share their curse."

Then she kissed him on the forehead, and she said, "Here, eat your lentil stew before it gets cold."

We know the choice Nicodemus made as well as the better circle of friends he chose to turn in, because we have this report from John 19:38-42:

> After [the crucifixion of Jesus], Joseph of Arimathea, being a disciple of Jesus, but secretly, for fear of the Jews, asked Pilate that he might take away the body of Jesus; and Pilate gave him permission.

> So he came and took the body of Jesus. And Nicodemus, who at first came to Jesus by night, also came, bringing a mixture of myrrh and aloes, about a hundred pounds. Then they took the body of Jesus, and bound it in strips of linen with the spices, as the custom of the Jews is to bury. Now in the place where he was crucified there was a garden, and in the garden a new tomb in which no one had yet been laid. So there they laid Jesus... for the tomb was nearby.

Earlier today we read from Paul's letter to the Romans that "Abraham *believed* God, and it was reckoned to him as righteousness." The promise that he would inherit the world did not come to Abraham or to his descendants through the law but through the righteousness of faith.

Paul says this righteousness is not just for the biological descendants of Abraham, but also to those who share the faith of Abraham. Just as being counted righteous by God took a leap of faith for Abraham—and for Nicodemus—so it will take a leap of faith for you.

For those who take that leap, the reward is spectacular—as Paul wrote (my paraphrase), "for we are not believing in the pharisaical scuttlebutt from around the water cooler, but in the God "who gives life to the dead, and who calls into existence the things that do not exist."

CLOSING HYMN: "The Solid Rock"

Stylistic Observations

The humor of imagining Nicodemus in a contemporary work setting, chatting it up with colleagues by the water cooler at breaktime, is designed to grab the imagination of the audience and help them relate to the conundrum faced by a man 2,000 years ago.

Most people will be able to relate to the writing technique used, that of "interior monologue" as the brilliant Nicodemus works his way through various passages of scripture to sort out the truth. This technique of presenting the biblical content is also far more interesting as it paraphrases and blends biblical texts in narrative fashion rather than a lecture style that tediously reviews bullet points.

The plot then segues from interior monologue to a warm dialogue between the scholar and his wife—and what a woman she is! "Poor Nicky! You are just going to have to make a decision, aren't you?" And then she jolts him out of his tortured thoughts and into action by kissing him on the forehead and ordering, "Here, eat your lentil stew before it gets cold."

The goal, of course, is to get the audience to experience the same faith and joy as Nicodemus finds when he comes to embrace with mind, heart, and soul, the God who gives life.

Your Notes:

_____

_____

_____

_____

_____

_____

Chapter 5: Easter

What Jesus Knew About Himself
(From Vol. 2: *Remembering the Story of God*)

CALL TO WORSHIP: Psalm 95:1-2

COLLECT: O God, whose blessed Son made himself known to his disciples in the breaking of bread: Open the eyes of our faith, that we may behold him in all his redeeming work; who lives and reigns with you, in the unity of the Holy Spirit, one God, now and for ever. Amen.

HYMN: "The Day of Resurrection"

NEW TESTAMENT: Remember this portion of the story of God from the Book we love found in Acts 2:14a,36-41.

RESPONSE: Psalm 116:1-3, 10-17

HYMN: "My Tribute"

PRAYER HYMN: "O Master, Let Me Walk with Thee"

PASTORAL PRAYER

THE LORD'S PRAYER

EPISTLE: Remember this teaching from the story of God in the Book we love found in 1 Peter 1:17-23.

THE GOSPEL: Remember this story of Jesus from the Book we love as recorded in Luke 24:13-35.

Homily: What Jesus Knew About Himself

It generally took Cleopas about two hours to walk the seven miles from his place in Emmaus up hill to Jerusalem. He generally clocked about a 15-minute mile, which left him an extra 15 minutes to stop and chat with neighbors, or to relax in a shady spot about half-way to take a swig from his flask and to munch on a few dates.

Going back to Emmaus was faster because it was more downhill, he liked to get home before dark, and the exercise device on his arm told him he was doing a comfortable 12-minute mile without even breaking a sweat.

Usually he didn't go alone—it was just safer to have a companion—so that sped up his pace if the other guy was a fast walker—or it slowed him down if it was his wife, because she had a shorter stride. But anyway, what's the hurry?

Especially on this sad day.

The injustice of a corrupt political system had recently executed their dear friend Jesus. It felt like the end of the world. So when Jesus himself came near and went with them, they didn't even look up. When he said to them, "What are you discussing?" they stood still.

Looking sad, Cleopas, answered him, telling the whole story while looking down and drawing a circle in the dirt with the toe of his sandal, even including the rumor that said Jesus of Nazareth had risen from the dead. In reply, Jesus told them they needed to believe all that the prophets had declared! Was it not necessary that the Messiah should suffer these things and then enter into his glory? Then, beginning with Moses, he interpreted to them the things written about himself.

Genesis 3:15 was where he started, explaining that because of original sin, God put enmity between the offspring of the woman and the serpent, "and the Messiah, born of a woman, will crush the serpent's head, and the serpent will strike his heel."

That happened.

Also mentioned by Moses in both Genesis 12:3 and Genesis 22:18 was that through the offspring of Abraham, all nations on earth will be blessed, "because you have *obeyed* me."

Jesus also pointed out Genesis 17:19 and Genesis 21:12 which specify that the Messiah will be a descendant of Isaac: "Your wife Sarah will bear you a son, and you will call him Isaac. I will establish my everlasting covenant with him."

For good measure, he threw in Genesis 49:10: "The scepter will not depart from Judah, nor the ruler's staff from between his feet, until he to whom it belongs shall come and the obedience of the nations shall be his."

Now Jesus looks beyond Genesis, scans his memory of all five books of Moses, and lands on Numbers 24:17 where it says, "A star will come out of Jacob; a scepter will rise out of Israel." And he reminds them of Deuteronomy 18:15 where Moses tells the people, "The Lord your God will raise up for you a prophet like me from among you, from your fellow Israelites. You must listen to him."

Cleopas and his companion glance at each other and say, "Yup—yup, that's an accurate lineage of Jesus of Nazareth all right—son of Abraham, son of Isaac, son of Jacob, son of Judah. For sure he was a prophet all right, and we listened to him."

As they come around the big boulder at the one mile marker where bandits like to loiter, Jesus says, "Of course, your friend Jesus of Nazareth might not be the right guy, because Micah 5:2 says the Messiah is to be born in Bethlehem: 'But you, Bethlehem Ephrathah, though you are small among the clans of Judah, out of you will come for me one who will be ruler over Israel, whose origins are from of old, from ancient times.'"

"That squares with the history we know," says the friend of Cleopas. "Jesus was born in Bethlehem—his parents were visiting there for the census when he was born—and then they fled to Egypt until Herod was dead. When they came back, he lived in Nazareth."

"Oh!" says Jesus. "Then he fulfilled two more prophecies: Hosea 11:1 says he would spend a season in Egypt, and Jeremiah 31:15 predicts a massacre of children at the time of the Messiah's birth.

"But the real question is," says Jesus, "What sort of lady was his mom? Because you'll remember what Isaiah (7:14) says, 'Therefore the Lord himself will give you a sign: The *virgin* will conceive and give birth to a son, and will call him Immanuel.'"

"We are personal friends with his mother, Mary," says Cleopas [tapping his chest with his left hand]. It's an amazing story, but we know it's true—she was in fact a virgin when the angel Gabriel appeared to her and she conceived her son Jesus."

"Cool," says Jesus. "That squares with something else Isaiah (11:1) says, "'He'll be called a Nazarene.'

"Tell you what, friends, we just strolled past mile marker two, so let me run some Psalms by you, and you tell me if they ring true of Jesus. Let's see, there's

- Psalm 2:6, the Messiah will be called King.
- Psalm 2:7, the Messiah will be the Son of God. [As Jesus talks, the listeners nod their heads and say things like, "Yeah, they called him that."]
- Psalm 8:2, the Messiah will be praised by little children. [Oh!—the kids loved him!]
- Psalm 22:7-8, the Messiah would be mocked and ridiculed. [Hail, king of the Jews!]
- Psalm 22:16, the Messiah's hands and feet would be pierced. [Jesus put his hands behind his back when he says that, and he's glad his sandals are of the type that hide the tops of his feet....]
- Psalm 22:18, soldiers will gamble for the Messiah's garments [They just nod as these images of the crucifixion flash through their minds.]
- Psalm 34:20, his bones would not be broken, just like the bones of the Passover sacrifice are not to be broken as it says in Exodus 12:46. [They did everything else you can imagine to torture him, but they never broke any bones.]

- Psalm 35:11, the Messiah will be falsely accused.
- Psalm 35:19 and Psalm 69:4, the Messiah will be hated without cause.
- Psalm 41:9, the Messiah will be betrayed. ["Judas," they mutter under their breath.]
- Psalm 69:8, he will be rejected by his own people.
- Psalm 69:21, the Messiah will be given vinegar to drink. [What?! It says that?! "Yes, my friend, it does say that: 'They put gall in my food and gave me vinegar for my thirst.'" [They shake their heads in amazement.]
- Jesus continues: Psalm 78-2-4 says he will speak in parables."

"No kidding?" These two people can't help themselves—they have strolled past two more mile markers by the time they finish giving Jesus a summary of all the parables Jesus told them: lost coin, prodigal son, Lazarus the beggar and the rich guy, 5, 2, & 1 talents....

Jesus just nods and listens—but as they're coming up on mile marker five Jesus has to interrupt them. He says, "We were in the Psalms, but let's make sure we don't miss what Isaiah said about the Messiah. Was he completely silent before his accusers?" [Yes—and Pilate was particularly surprised by this.]

"Did anybody spit on or strike your friend? Because Isaiah 50:6 says that would happen. [They sure did.]

"Was he crucified all alone or with criminals—I only ask because it does say in Isaiah 53:12 that he poured out his life unto death and was numbered with the transgressors." ["One criminal was crucified on his right, another on his left," they replied.]

"He didn't happen to be buried with the rich, did he? Because that's predicted in Isaiah 53:9." [Cleopas says, "our very successful colleague Joseph of Arimathea buried Jesus in a new tomb hollowed out from a rock and used 100 pounds of embalming ointments supplied by Nicodemus, a member of the ruling class of Pharisees."]

They are walking a little faster now, and the two disciples seem to be experiencing something like fire in their hearts—but not the kind that comes from the exhaustion of running too fast.

"Now then," says Jesus—almost as if he were a Rabbi used to teaching the scriptures while walking to different places with students. "Let's think about what *Zechariah* had to say about the Messiah. He says in chapter 11:12-13 that he will be betrayed and that his price money will be used to buy a potter's field, and he says in the next chapter—chapter 12:10, that soldiers will pierce his side." ["You're talking about Judas, and the soldier at the crucifixion with the spear," they reply.]

"So far, so good," says Jesus as they walk past mile marker six. "Now comes the really tough part. Psalm 109:4 says the Messiah will pray for his enemies...." ["He did!" they almost yell—just before he died, he said, "Father, forgive them—they don't know what they're doing!"]

"My dear friends," says Jesus. "It sounds to me like you have a serious candidate for Messiah on your hands. But here's where the leather hits the road— Psalm 16:10 and Psalm 49:15 both say that the Messiah will resurrect from the dead—and just a few miles back you were telling me that Jesus of Nazareth was reported to have been raised from the dead—or did I hear you wrong?" [Their eyes are WIDE open now and they're both thinking, "You mean maybe it could possibly, actually, certifiably be true?"]

Jesus smiles and says, "Well then, if the Psalm was right about him rising from the dead, maybe Psalm 110:4 is also right—that he will be a prophet, priest, and king—all three, just like Melchizedek. And then there's Psalm 24:7-10, that he will ascend into heaven. And then we are told in Psalm 110:1 that he will be seated at God's right hand."

They are just coming up to Cleopas's front door now, and Jesus acts as if he intends to go further, but they implore him to stay with them, and they offer him supper.

As they go in the house and remove their sandals, Jesus says, "I saved one of my favorite prophecies for this moment. It says in Psalm 61:1-2, 'He will be sent to heal the brokenhearted.' I predict that you folks will experience healing for your broken hearts—probably a lot sooner than you can imagine!"

Just a few minutes later he breaks the bread— and they *see his hands*—last time they saw those hands they had spikes right through them and into a wooden crossbeam—and they recognize him—they truly SAW him!—and then he disappeared.

MEDITATION: "Come to Us, Beloved Stranger"

Stylistic Observations

Rather than telling *the audience Jesus knew he was the Messiah, this homily* shows *that he obviously knew he was and allows them to draw the correct conclusion using their own powers of reasoning.*

Hemingway carried over into his fiction the newspaper-reporter discipline of using only the word "said" in attribution and set the model for this dialogue in which I wish to keep my own spin absolutely out of sight and let the powerful proofs of Scripture shine in all their power.

An otherwise didactic blast of facts and lists and proof texts comes alive by placing them in this brisk style of dialogue between "interlocutors" as was done by the Early Modern English writer John Bunyan in The Life and Death of Mr. Badman. *But they wrote mainly in the past tense 300 years ago, and placing the dialogue in present tense gives the scene a modern feel made popular by Damon Runyon in the 20th century.*

Your Notes:

_____

_____

_____

_____

_____

_____

Chapter 6: Ascension

God took a Body
(From Vol. 1: *Rehearsing the Story of God*)

CALL TO WORSHIP: Psalm 47

THE COLLECT: Almighty God, whose blessed Son our Savior Jesus Christ ascended far above all heavens that he might fill all things: Mercifully give us faith to perceive that, according to His promise, He abides with His Church on earth, even to the end of the ages; through Jesus Christ our Lord, who lives and reigns with You and the Holy Spirit, one God, in glory everlasting. Amen.

HYMN: "Crown Him with Many Crowns"

THE GOSPEL: Luke 24:44-53

EPISTLE: Ephesians 1:15-23

HYMN: "Hail the Day That Sees Him Rise"

PRAYER HYMN: "Christ Is Made the Sure Foundation"

PASTORAL PRAYER

THE LORD'S PRAYER

NEW TESTAMENT: Acts 1:1-11

Homily: God Took a Body
The word *ascension* refers to the elevation of Christ into heaven by his own power in the presence of his disciples the 40th day after his resurrection.

Since Easter is always on a Sunday and the Ascension is 40 days later, it is *never* on a Sunday—always on a Thursday!—so it tends to be ignored. That's unfortunate since in fact it may be the most important event in the history of the world.

When it is observed, the day is generally depicted as a time to celebrate his completion of the work of our salvation, his pledge that we will one day be glorified with Christ, and his entry into heaven carrying his humanity with him.

To help us dig into what this actually means, with Renée's permission, I have borrowed some information from the first 10 pages of a 42-page paper she wrote on the Ascension as part of her doctoral program. She writes that Luke reveals in chapter 24:25-27 and 44-49 some of the things Jesus taught during the 40 days he appeared post-resurrection to the apostles. Jesus validated his Messiahship, interpreted the Old Testament prophesies regarding his resurrection, and he instructed his disciples on their responsibility to be his witnesses of all that had happened, what Jesus had taught them, and what they were to do next.

As opposed to Jesus' transfiguration which had only three witnesses, a large group of people witnessed his ascension. The Transfiguration was essentially a preparatory event for the disciples as it pointed toward "the coming exaltation and fulfillment of Christ's ministry."

If you've been keeping up on your Church

history, you might remember Lactantius [Lack-TAN-shus] who lived to be 80 years old and died in 320 AD. He was an advisor to Roman emperor Constantine who had become a Christian. Here's my modern paraphrase of what Lactantius had to say about the ascension in his *Epitome of the Divine Institutes*:

After his resurrection, Jesus went into Galilee, re-assembled his disciples who had fled through fear, and gave them commands which he wished to be observed. Then, having arranged for the preaching of the gospel throughout the whole world, he breathed into them the Holy Spirit, and gave them the power to work miracles. On the 40th day he returned to his Father, being carried up into a cloud.

The prophet Daniel had long before shown this, saying, "I saw in the night vision one like the Son of man came with the clouds of heaven, and came to the Ancient of days; and they who stood beside him brought him near before him. And there was given him a kingdom, and glory, and dominion, and all people, tribes, and languages shall serve him; and his power is an everlasting one, which shall not pass away, and his kingdom that which shall not be destroyed."

David also foresaw this and wrote in the sixth Psalm: "The Lord said unto my Lord, Sit Thou at my right hand, until I make Thine enemies Thy footstool."

Luke's description of Jesus as he left the earth shows the disciples looking into the sky, rather than all around them, indicating that

Jesus appeared to go up, instead of merely disappearing. The cloud that hid him may have been the cloud of God's glory, similar to that which appeared during all those long years of wandering in the wilderness on their journey from Egypt to the Promised Land.

A similar cloud appeared at Jesus' transfiguration, and signified God's approval of his Son. God's *shekinah*, the visible presence of his glory, is made known by the cloud—the same kind of cloud seen in connection with the tabernacle during the wilderness wanderings that represented God's dwelling-place. The angels' message made it known to the disciples that Jesus now had a new, heavenly existence.

Two prominent biblical theological interpretations of the Ascension appear in Hebrews and Ephesians. Hebrews 8-10 presents Jesus as our High Priest and compares his work with that of the high priest in the Old Testament temple. As the high priest entered the Holy of Holies in order to present sacrifices for the sins of the people once per year, Christ, "entered once for all time into the most holy place—entering, not with the blood of goats or calves or some other prescribed animal, but offering his own blood and thus obtaining redemption for us for all time" (Hebrews 9:12 *The Voice*).

Not only did Jesus become a sacrifice for sin in a new covenant which made the former covenant obsolete as described in Hebrews 8:13, there is more to the story. Jesus continues his work as our eternal intercessor by means of his ascension: "Therefore he is able to save completely those who come to God through him, *because he always lives to intercede for them*" (Heb. 7:25 NIV).

Jesus was a sinless human being and, through faith, we are united with him, and, therefore, the day will come when we can also be raised to the throne of God with him.

Also, in Acts 1:5 and 8-9, Jesus connected his ascension to the sending of the Holy Spirit. The signs of the Spirit at work in his church are evidence of the presence of the ascended Christ.

A few examples include Matthew 18:20, informing us that "where two or three are gathered in my name, there am I in the midst of them," our invitation to identify with the death and resurrection of Christ through baptism as mentioned in Romans 6:1-11, and of course whenever we partake of his presence in the Eucharistic elements as explained in John 6:25-59.

In about 460 AD, Pope Leo the Great felt motivated to write Sermon 73, a rousing admonition that helps us appreciate the significance of the ascension. He said:

> The Apostles and all the disciples, who were bewildered at his death and slow to believe his resurrection, were so strengthened by the clearness of the truth that when the Lord entered the heights of heaven, not only were they affected with no sadness, but were even filled with great joy.

And truly great and unspeakable was their cause for joy, when in the sight of the holy multitude, above the dignity of all heavenly creatures, the *Nature* of mankind went up, to pass above the angels' ranks and to rise beyond the archangels' heights, and to have its uplifting limited by no elevation until, received to sit with the Eternal Father, it should be associated on the throne with his glory, to whose *Nature* it was united in the Son.

Since then Christ's ascension is our uplifting, and the hope of the body is raised, whither the glory of the Head has gone before, let us exult, dearly-beloved, with worthy joy and delight in the loyal paying of thanks.

What does this mean, that "*the Nature of mankind went up*"? Let's back up and get the full picture. Through the Incarnation, God *became* his creation. As far as we were previously told, God is spirit, not matter. He created the galaxies and all the material Universe.

We have amazing telescopes now and can look light-years into the past by means of astronomy and can just begin to fathom the magnitude of God's creation.

Then he created *life*—a big improvement over lifeless rocks. He took the dust he had made and added nerves and blood vessels and brain cells and lungs and hearts—he breathed into it the breath of life, and clay came alive!

Inconceivable! God not only made life, he made it

conceivable—capable of conceiving and producing on-going life—every creature after its kind—DNA and the propagation of the species!

In addition to telescopes, now we have microscopes and can look at amazingly tiny things—and we're seeing that these tiny things we call "cells" are actually miniature galaxies! The nucleus is like a sun with planets of electrons and protons and neutrons orbiting them, and neutrinos streaming through them, and—and—and—how can I explain this?

Suffice it to say that your body is the most incredible creation in the history of—*history*. That human body is the climax of God's creative efforts.

No wonder Satan desired to corrupt it.

No wonder God fully intends to redeem it—so much so that he placed himself into one of those bodies. In that capacity he became sin for us, paid the penalty for sin, rose from the dead, and then—and then—and this is why the Ascension is such a big deal—and then he returned to heaven—taking his human body with him!

God is forever different now.

God left heaven without a body—God is spirit.

God then took a body.

And when he rose from the dead and returned to heaven, he took his body back to heaven with him.

It's not just a metaphor anymore. Now Jesus *physically* sits at the right hand of God the Father.

All the kingdoms of this world that Satan offered him during that temptation in the wilderness have now been given to him by their rightful owner.

Christ's *continuing* incarnation is a crucial tenet of the Christian faith and a great pity if you have not heard it explained before. Jesus became, and remains, our brother *in the flesh*, and his presence in heaven should dramatically affect how we see our lives and place in the world today. We who have received Christ can participate with him, by means of his and our unity with the Spirit, in his resurrection, ascension, and being seated at God's right hand.

Tertullian affirmed:

> Jesus is still sitting there at the right hand of the Father, man, yet God—the last Adam, yet the primary Word—flesh and blood, yet purer than ours—who "shall descend in like manner as he ascended into heaven." He keeps in his own self the deposit of the flesh which has been committed to him by both parties—the pledge and security of its entire perfection.

We in the *present tense* are already participating in the Kingdom of God! The verb tenses of Scripture ring true: "You <u>have been</u> raised with Christ" (Colossians 3:1 NIV), and "God raised us up with Christ and seated us with him in the heavenly realms in Christ Jesus" (Ephesians 2:6 NIV).

God took a body—*and kept it.* Therefore, the kingdoms of this world are become the kingdom of our Lord and of his Christ. And he shall reign for ever and ever.

Welcome to the Kingdom of Heaven.

HYMN: "Rejoice the Lord is King!"

Stylistic Observations

This homily sidesteps the teaching and argumentative mode in favor of a stance more of wonderment and amazement at the magnitude of what God was actually doing when he became human. The plot builds breathlessly to its astonishing climax that Jesus is now and forever a physical being.

The presentation uses in a historically sequential way the Wesleyan Quadrilateral by taking information from Scripture, History, Tradition, and Reason to overwhelm the audience with powerful insights into what the Incarnation means to God as well as to believers. Deliberately nondenominational, it references not only the prophets and apostles, but church fathers from Lactantius to Pope Leo, as well as modern scientific references (DNA) to portray a compelling and universal truth about God.

Your Notes:

_____

_____

_____

_____

_____

_____

Chapter 7: Pentecost

Chimeras of God
(From Vol. 3: *Receiving the Story of God*)

CALL TO WORSHIP from Psalm 28:1-2, 6-7

HYMN: "I Will Praise Him"

COLLECT: O God, from whom all good proceeds: Grant that by your inspiration we may think those things that are right, and by your merciful guiding may do them; through Jesus Christ our Lord, who lives and reigns with you and the Holy Spirit, one God, for ever and ever. Amen.

HYMN: "Seek Ye First"

OLD TESTAMENT: Receive this troubling account of the original sin as recorded in the Story of God as found in Genesis 3:8-15.

HYMN: "There's a Wideness in God's Mercy

PRAYER HYMN: "Take My Life and Let It Be"

PASTORAL PRAYER

THE LORD'S PRAYER

MUSICAL MEDITATION: "I Lift My Eyes" (Psalm 121)

EPISTLE: Receive this teaching from the Book we love as presented in 2 Corinthians 4:13-5:1.

THE GOSPEL: Receive this insight from Jesus into the nature of his kingdom as is recorded in Mark 3:20-35.

Homily: Chimeras of God

On this second Sunday after Pentecost, the Church is grappling with an incredibly powerful transformation that has taken place in the story of humanity. To put this transformation into context we read first a short portion of the story of original sin—the part where the deceiving serpent loses its legs, and its entire species is forever condemned to crawling on its belly and eating dust.

What a mystery this must have been for our grandparents and their ancestors over the past 4,000 years. When they read this passage from the Story of God, how could they possibly understand exactly what God did when he altered the genetic code of the creature that deceived Eve such it would lose its legs, and none of its descendants could grow legs? What did they think?

"When I was a boy," says a shepherd from ancient times when delving into this mystery, "a stray sheep got a leg amputated by a predator before I could rescue it. But a year later it got pregnant with twins—and both lambs were born with four perfectly fine legs! So this thing God did to the serpent must be different from that—more permanent."

"Exactly!" says the second guy sitting by the fire. "Same thing happened to my Uncle Eli's dog Shep— she lost a leg and later had a whole litter of four-legged whelps! So what God did to that serpent didn't just hurt him, but his entire species—must be some sort of miracle."

"I got one even better," says a third guy standing in the shadows whose eyes are fixed on the stars but whose ears are carefully listening. "You remember my older sister Rhoda? She never had no right hand for so long as I knowed her. But now she's got six kids with right hands and a whole passel of grandkids with right hands. If what God did to the serpent is normal, seems like it would apply everywhere— seems like all Rhoda's kids would only have a left hand...."

"So then," says the first shepherd, "It's a proven fact—you can change an animal, but you have not changed its genetic code...."

"I ain't never heard that word 'genetic code,'" says the shepherd in the dark. "Where'd you get that?"

Not until 1904 would a Russian physicist named Georgiy Gamov coin the term "genetic code," and in the century that followed, humans took giant strides in understanding the precise techniques God may have used in doing some of his miracles. Using the same knowledge he used to create the serpent creature's original DNA, he altered its essential nature to be forever legless.

Similarly, because of original sin as narrated in the same scripture passage, God appears to have taken out the biological eternal life code in the DNA of humans while leaving their minds ever-longing for the recovery of this loss. Our bodies endlessly strive for healing even as they relentlessly crumble away.

In our second portion of Scripture, Paul explains to the Corinthians that the gift of the Holy Spirit at Pentecost forever changes the spiritual DNA of those who believe and receive Him. He says, "we know that the one who raised the Lord Jesus will raise us also with Jesus…. So we do not lose heart. Even though our outer nature is wasting away, our inner nature is being renewed day by day. For this slight momentary affliction is preparing us for an eternal weight of glory beyond all measure…. For we know that if the earthly tent we live in is destroyed, we have a building from God, a house not made with hands, eternal in the heavens."

Is this farfetched—for me to hint at the possibility that modern-day, Spirit-filled followers of Jesus are genetically modified organisms—or as I called it in the title of this homily, "Chimeras" of God?

The August 8, 2016, issue of *Scientific American* published a fascinating article called "Three Human Chimeras that Already Exist." The article says a "chimera" is a single organism having two sets of DNA. This happens when one fraternal twin dies very soon after conception and some of its cells are absorbed by the other twin.

It can also happen when a person has a bone marrow transplant. The new bone marrow stem cells develop into red blood cells, and for the rest of the patient's life, that person will have some blood cells that are genetically different from the other cells in his body.

The third type of chimera is represented by at least half of the people in this room. If you are a woman who has ever been pregnant, you might be a chimera. The article says we know this because of a 2015 research study that tested tissue samples from multiple organs of 26 women who died while pregnant or shortly after giving birth. Cells containing the babies' DNA were found in all of these organs, and they were definitely fetus cells because they contained a Y chromosome (found only in males) and the babies were all boys. Of course—you may have suspected this—the mothers were all females.

Recently Renée and I started subscribing to the *Smithsonian* magazine, and the May 2021 issue contains an article called "The Making of a Mom" that explains how an unborn child can literally shape a mother's heart and mind. Listen to this sentence from page 52 of that article:

> A mother's body is like her living room, strewn with kid castoffs and debris…. Our children colonize our lungs, spleens, kidneys, thyroids, skin. Their cells embed in our bone marrow and breasts. Often they stay forever. Scientists find rogue fetal cells while autopsying the cadavers of old women, whose babies are now middle-aged. Long after giving birth, the bodies of surrogate mothers are scattered with the genes of strangers' progeny.

But the article is mainly about how a woman's heart and mind turns toward her child after she conceives.

Hard science at Emory University studied the biochemical changes that abruptly renovate a pregnant woman's mind toward a tender maternal instinct such that "old systems of desire have been rewired." The author writes, "The most striking change in motherhood isn't about how we look on the outside. It's about how we see."

The hormone Oxytocin does not just flood the bloodstream to prepare a woman's body to give birth, it is also called the "love hormone" or the "trust hormone" that transforms a woman's brain. In one study they had women with no children snort puffs of oxytocin and they suddenly became responsive and sensitive to baby faces and the crying or laughing of infants.

Maybe they should put that stuff in an aerosol bottle so a woman can spray it around the room a few minutes before announcing to her husband that she is pregnant.

That word "chimera" has been around for a long time. It describes creatures that have a dual nature—a mixture of multiple parts of other species, such as Homer's description of a beast in the *Iliad* that was part lion, part serpent, and part goat, or the Carchemish Chimera that is a winged lion that also has a human head.

The Egyptian Sphinx is variously portrayed with the head of a human, a falcon, a cat, or a sheep, and the body of a lion with the wings of a falcon.

Hydra is a gigantic water-snake-like monster with nine heads.

Pegasus is a white horse with the wings of a huge bird.

Geryon in Dante's *Inferno* is a giant of a man with three heads, sometimes also depicted as having three bodies.

Beyond mythology, we now know that the oceans are swimming with Chimera forms known informally as ghost sharks, rat fish, spook fish, or rabbit fish.

Children these days have no trouble at all believing in such things because they are growing up watching something called "animation" on television. Animals speak and act like humans. A frog on Sesame Street falls in love with a pig. A green creature named Oscar of indefinite progeny but distinct Muppet characteristics exhibits a grouchy disposition.

By now your mind has probably turned to that chimera in the Bible that plays a major role in last things. In Revelation 12:3 we can meet an enormous red dragon with seven heads and ten horns and seven crowns on its heads. A similar beast is depicted in Revelation 17:3 where we see a woman sitting on a scarlet beast that is covered with blasphemous names and has seven heads and ten horns.

Now that we think of it, it's obvious that our world is full of the notion of the chimera, so it's not fantastical for Christians to believe that Jesus is both fully God and fully Man.

And it's not fantastical to believe that a mortal human being can be filled with the eternal Holy Spirit of Jesus and have both a transformed mind and the hope of a transfigured body fully capable of resurrection from the dead and eternal life by the power of the God who first formed it from the dust of the ground and breathed into it the breath of life.

This may be the spiritual sort of DNA Jesus was talking about in the very contentious gospel passage we read where he is being accused of having the power to cast out demons because he himself is demon possessed.

He sternly explains to these people that not only is their logic flawed—how can Satan cast out Satan? Indeed, someone stronger has entered Satan's house and is plundering his property.

Not only is their logic flawed, their souls are in peril for they are on the cusp of committing the unforgivable sin of blaspheming against the Holy Spirit.

When his biological mother and siblings arrive on the scene, Jesus redirects the crowd's thinking toward some sort of spiritual DNA with redemptive eternal consequences. He looks at those seated around him and says, "<u>Here</u> are my mother and my brothers! Whoever does the will of God <u>is</u> my brother and sister and mother."

The language of the Bible is infused with this innate awareness of redemption DNA:

You must be born again. WHAT? Do you mean literally, or is that just a metaphor?

I will remove your heart of stone and give you a heart of flesh. WHAT? Do you mean literally, or is that just a metaphor?

You can be filled with all the fullness of God. WHAT? Do you mean literally, or is that just a metaphor?

You can be born of the flesh and of the Holy Spirit. WHAT? Do you mean literally, or is that just a metaphor?

That endless debate about transubstantiation may come into play here. Do the bread and wine of communion somehow contain the actual DNA of the human Jesus? What did Jesus know that his disciples could not comprehend when he said, "this is my body broken for you; this is my blood shed for the remission of your sins"? WHAT? Do you mean literally, or is that just a metaphor?

The carefully worded Protestant liturgy we use in an interdenominational service of worship embraces this mystery—no matter whether participants at the communion table believe in the literal or the metaphorical interpretation—by praying that this bread and wine may "become for us" the body and blood of Christ.

We say it is "because of the *mystery of the Word made flesh*" that God has caused a new light to shine in our hearts.

Therefore, in remembrance and in celebration, we eat the bread and drink from the cup, and we proclaim the *mystery* of faith: Christ has died. Christ is risen. Christ will come again.

And we say that *by definition* the Church is the body of Christ.

If the expression I've been using, "WHAT? Do you mean literally, or is that just a metaphor?" annoys you, maybe it's because you were paying attention in your literature class where it was hopefully explained that the very reason we use metaphors at all is because a metaphor is about the only mental tool we have for explaining what is otherwise incomprehensible. We use metaphors to explore a deeper, otherwise unknowable physical reality.

Modern science is fascinating precisely because it is beginning to discover HOW God does some of the things he does. It's easier to believe in him once we see that what we thought was magic is really a genius mind at work doing science we call miracles. We understand that all of life is miraculous, that God is the miracle worker, and that he wants to miraculously transform us so that we can participate more fully with him in the ongoing miracle of redemption for all of creation.

Remember those ancient shepherds who we heard earlier as they tried to solve the mystery of how God delt with the deceiving serpent in the creation story? Well, now it's a couple thousand years later, and we see their genetically identical great, great, great, great grandchildren still working as shepherds out on the hills surrounding Jerusalem. It's a week after Pentecost, the word is out that more unusual things have happened, and these shepherds are still having the same, centuries-old conversation.

A disciple of Jesus has come by to say, "Christ in you is your hope of glory."

After he leaves, one shepherd thinks out loud, "Where in you is he?"

"He's in your heart," says shepherd two. "Or maybe he's in your mind."

A third shepherd standing nearby gazing out at the gathering clouds but listening carefully says, "Maybe it means Christ is in your soul."

Shepherd one replies, "You're both right. You receive Christ into your genetic code."

"I ain't never heard that word 'genetic code,'" says the shepherd in the dark. "Where'd you get that?"

"I don't know," says shepherd one. "Maybe it's just a part of my DNA...."

It sounds kooky, but it keeps happening. It happened at Pentecost when the story of God transmogrified into the story of humanity. Jesus the God-Man is making us like himself—we are being transformed into the image of God—growing new heads where needed—breathing fire where appropriate—blanketing the planet with hope and grace and mercy and love and all the fruit of the Spirit that grow naturally in the lives of anyone possessing his DNA.

Indeed, that is the job description of all these millions of genetically modified followers of Jesus— to be Chimeras of God.

The end of the world is upon us, and just in time, by the mercy and eternal plan of God, we have been given precisely the DNA we need to adapt from the sentence of death to the promise of eternal life—and to take along with us all those who are likewise being saved.

HYMN: "O to Be Like Thee!"
BENEDICTION: Ephesians 3:20-21

Stylistic Observations

This homily relies on the intrigue of the word "Chimeras" to grab audience interest, and when the narrative starts to get boring with too much scientific material, the plot takes over with the entertainment provided by colloquial dialog of imaginary shepherds. The fact that they turn up again at the conclusion gives the somewhat humorous feel of the homily a fitting punchline.

Repetition of the interjection "WHAT? Do you mean literally, or is that just a metaphor?" is a rhetorical device for adding to the humor and keeping the audience awake while also teaching an important lesson on how to read, understand, and correctly interpret God's Word.

Your Notes:

_____

_____

_____

_____

_____

_____